ANIMALS AND THEIR BABIES
Pigs and Piglets

written by Anita Ganeri

illustrated by Anni Axworthy

CHERRYTREE BOOKS

A Cherrytree book

Published by
Evans Publishing Group
2A Portman Mansions
Chiltern St
London W1U 6NR

© Evans Brothers Limited 2007
Text © Anita Ganeri 2007

First published in 2007

Printed in China by WKT Co Ltd

British Library Cataloguing in Publication Data
Ganeri, Anita, 1961-
    Pigs and piglets. - (Animals and their babies)
    1. Piglets - Juvenile literature 2. Swine - Life cycles -
    Juvenile literature
    I. Title
    599.6'33156

ISBN 978184 234442 2

CONTENTS

New piglets   6

Drinking milk   8

Solid food   11

An outdoor life   12

Hungry piglets   14

Piglet shelter   16

Piglet showers   18

Grown-up pigs   20

Index   22

Further Information   22

A baby pig is called a piglet. Piglets grow inside their mother's body until they are ready to be born. Then the mother pig goes inside her hut and makes a cosy nest from straw.

The mother pig lies down in the straw. She has about eight to ten piglets at one time. The piglets are tiny, with twitching snouts and curly tails.

The piglets and their mother stay in the hut for two to three weeks. During this time, the piglets drink lots of their mother's milk. It is full of goodness to help them grow quickly.

The mother pig lies on her side while the piglets are drinking. They have to be careful not to get squashed if she shuffles and moves about.

The piglets spend most of their time drinking milk and sleeping. They also like to play and explore. They make lots of grunts, squeaks and squeals as they play.

When they are about two months old, the piglets stop drinking their mother's milk. The farmer starts to give them special dry, crusty piglet food to eat.

Now the piglets are old enough to live outside. They live with their brothers and sisters in a grassy field. They spend the day playing and chasing each other round and round.

The mother pig keeps a close eye on her piglets. If she sees danger, she gives a loud grunt to call the piglets to her.

Then they trot along beside her for safety.

As they get older, the farmer gives the piglets a different dry food to eat. It is made from grains like corn. The piglets also love eating scraps of bread and vegetables.

In their field, the piglets use their snuffly snouts to find food in the soil. Roots, acorns and juicy worms are tasty snacks for piglets.

The piglets don't live with their mother any more. They have their own hut. At night, they snuggle down in the straw. The straw makes a cosy bed.

The hut helps to keep the piglets snug and dry when it is bad weather outside. And when it is sunny, the hut is a shady place to hide in.

In very warm weather, the piglets can get very
hot. So the farmer sprays them with water to cool
them down. It is like having a pig shower.

But best of all, the piglets like to roll around in thick, gooey mud. The mud helps to keep them cool. It also stops them getting sunburnt.

The piglets are a year old. They are grown up. A male pig is called a boar. A female pig is called a sow. Pigs can live a long time, sometimes for up to 15 years.

The pigs are old enough to have their own piglets.
A male pig meets a female pig. A few months later,
the female pig has piglets. And the piglets will
grow into...new pigs!

Index

Boars (male pigs) 20

Huts 6, 8, 16, 17

Mating 21

Mother pig 6, 7, 8, 9, 13

Mud bath 19

Piglets 6
    birth of 7, 21
    drinking milk 8, 9, 10, 11
    living outside 12
    making noises 10
    playing 10, 12
    solid food 11, 14, 15

Showers 18

Sows (female pigs) 20

Sunburn 19

Further Information

To find out more about the lives of pigs and other farmyard animals, you can visit www.rspca.org.uk (the website of the Royal Society for the Prevention of Cruelty to Animals).